The Highest Honor

The Highest Honor

Don McCormick

The Highest Honor
Poems of Faith, Hope, and Love
Don McCormick

Copyright © 2013 Don McCormick

Edited by Amy S. Spencer. Edit United, Kalona, Iowa

ISBN-1O: 1484805232

ISBN-13: 978-14848O5237

Printed in the United States of America

First Edition: 6/2O13

To Mary, who still lives in my heart!

CONTENTS

THE HIGHEST HONOR

The military has always tried to honor those brave ones who have distinguished themselves on the field of battle. Some, of course, are never recognized, while others receive their recognition much later—some even posthumously (after they are dead). The scene we are about to witness is a little of both.

Seems impossible? Let's watch!

The highest-ranking officers of all the services are standing on the platform, their stars shining in the brilliance of a whole New Day. No one is in a hurry, for a change; since *it is a day that will never end.* Anyway, on with the story.

With them on the platform is the *honoree*. This Man, a Galilean, is distinguished by the fact that He is wearing a white robe and sandals and also, unknown to all, He is restraining some of the glow of His presence, so as not to overwhelm the proceedings. Now, who has something to say about this Man?

Officer 1: I do! I think it is very important to identify the One we honor today. Sir, in addition to the honor bestowed upon You by Your Father, for being an obedient son and for being like Him, we wish to bestow upon You a name also, for being like us. The name we give you is *Emmanuel*. Do you like it?

He: Yes, I like it very much.

   (The next officer steps forward and salutes.)

Officer 2: Sir, quite frankly, I was expecting these awards to be given posthumously. I heard You had died in the battle, but I am glad You were able to appear before us—and quite suddenly, I might add.

He: I am glad to be here with you. I wouldn't miss it for the world!

Officer 2: I see, also, that you brought some others with you. Let's see how many. The light is so bright...but it looks like...wait. (Pause.) It's a multitude, which no man can number! And they seem to come from every tribe and nation on Earth.

1

He: *Yes*, that is true.

Officer 2: One more question: How did they get their robes so white?

He: Well, they have washed their robes in the blood of the Lamb, you see.

Officer 2: Blood? Hmm, blood. OK, whatever You say. Someone else should say something, please. How about you? You are a heavy-weapons specialist, aren't you?

Specialist: Yes, I am, but I have some unanswered questions, too, about Your very effective use of weapons on the battlefield. Sir, the weapons You used were unique to the type of warfare you were facing—is that true?

He: Yes, very unique.

Specialist: You seemed not to battle against flesh and blood, but against principalities and powers and against wickedness in high places. What kind of weapons were they?

He: Well, they are not easy to describe, but one thing is sure: our weapons were not carnal, but were mighty through God to the pulling down of strongholds.

Specialist: Hmm! No kidding? Well, Sir, the reports I received from eye witnesses is that You did a great job. You did not regard Your own life dear to Yourself, but were willing to lay down Your life for others. Is this true?

He: Their word is true.

Specialist: Some say You did lay Your life down, but then, there are always conflicting reports. Reports! Reports! They are so unreliable at times. I wish I had seen it for myself. But I do see that You have some wounds in Your hands and some on Your feet as well. It looks like the enemy just about got You a few times. Is that true?

He: Oh, no, Sir, that is not true! "These wounds I received in the house of My friends."

Specialist: Your friends? What kind of friends are they?

He: Well, Sir, they did hide their faces from Me at one time, but now look at them. Aren't they beautiful?

Specialist: Ahem, I guess You could say that. Anyway, we are glad You did not lose Your life.

He: If I did lose My life, I certainly found it again, as you see. We can talk later, OK?

Specialist: OK, Mr. Emmanuel, later.

(Specialist goes back to his place on the platform.)

Officer 1: Could You tell us about Your biggest or most important battle?

He: It probably was related to the very reason for My first Coming.

Officer 1: Your first Coming?

He: Yes. I was trying to reach the top of this hill, called Calvary. It was not an inspiring sight, since it was shaped like a skull. It was the greatest objective of My entire life. But I kept falling down.

Officer 1: Falling down? Why?

He: Well, it was partly due to the loss of blood. I took some lashes on My back for My comrades in arms. I was also made to wear a crown made of thorns, but mostly My assault on Mount Calvary had to do with the heavy weapon I was carrying on My back. If that dark-complected fellow had not come along and carried it the rest of the way, I might not have made it. He deserves a medal, don't you think?

Officer 2: Who was it?

He: His name is Simon of Cyrene. Look! Up there, singing with everyone else. Stand up, Simon. Stand up! You are a true brother, and I am proud of you. You did a great job. A great job!

Officer 2: So Calvary was sort of the turning point, You say?

He: Yes, It was pretty lonely up there on top of that mountain. There were two other guys there, but their situation was no better than Mine. One of them did cry out to Me to remember him. I did, and he's up there sitting next to Simon.

3

Officer 1: I hear You lost more blood there. Did You?

He: Yes.

Officer 1: And did You recover soon?

He: Well, not really. You see, I was totally out of it for three days. The next thing I knew, it was resurrection morning. Yes, I know, that is a little difficult to explain. But there I was, out of bed, walking around in this little garden, feeling fine. Can you believe that?

Officer 1: At this point I can believe most anything! But right now that music coming from all those people is really getting to me. It seems like I could join in a little bit. Maybe I will just lift my hands, like this, and hum along with them.

He: A good idea. And I see you have run out of questions.

Officer 2: Sir, I have also been listening to that music—

Officer 1: Excuse me, but they like to call it worship, you know, to be accurate and all.

Officer 2: Yes. Worship. You're right, and do you hear the words they are saying? And they are about this Man, this Galilean, Emmanuel, here. They are saying, "Worthy is the Lamb that was slain and has redeemed us through God's mighty power; to receive power and riches and wisdom and strength and honor and glory and blessing."

Officer 1: I understand the report a little better now. Incredible though it may seem that I would believe such a thing. I perceive that You really did lay Your life down, but You actually took it up again. This, in itself, was the victory for us, and the defeat of our enemy!

He: You're getting there, aren't you? And prophecy instead of questions—I can go for that any time.

Officer 1: We really do want to get on with the business at hand, but have you noticed how the level has changed since we first started?

Officer 2: It really has come up. Maybe there is no limit. What do you think?

Officer 1: There don't appear to be limits anymore. I would just like to know how we got to this day. What made it happen, anyway? And why is so much light coming from those two sitting over there? It is almost blinding us. And why is the third seat empty?

He: I meant to talk to them about the light, but you see the tall one? That is Gabriel. He stood with one foot on the land and one foot on the sea, and he swore that delay was no longer to be. So, here we are!

Officer 1: That is a lot to think about. What about the other one?

He: The other one is Michael. He has just finished binding our great adversary—the devil, Satan—and has cast him into the bottomless pit.

Officer 2: You're kidding! A bottomless pit? Oh, oh, yes! I believe you! What about the empty seat?

He: That seat is empty because the Adversary was not always that way. At one time he was Lucifer, an angel. He was strong, beautiful, powerful, full of light, and he had almost everything. But he became arrogant. He wanted the Highest place. He was ready to exalt himself. That was a big mistake. Therefore, he was cast down into darkness. That seat would have been his today, if he hadn't messed up.

Officer 2: Hmm, I'll bet he caused a lot of other wars too.

He: Yes, and he hindered so many people from doing what they were sent to do. Some overcame; some didn't. These down here on the front seats know about that. There is Paul, Timothy, Moses, Elijah, JRS, and many more. OK, G and M, APCO, John and Chris—all the others too. You get the picture, don't you?

Officer 2: Sure do! Say, can we do a couple more things here. There are a lot of the kings of the Earth present today and other people with crowns. Here are the four and twenty elders with theirs, and Paul with his crown of righteousness. And Stephen with his martyr's crown. Since we aren't going to be studying war anymore, we have taken all our stars and gold braid and have made them into a crown. We want You to be crowned with many crowns. Here, wear this one for all the victories You have caused to be won. Like they are singing, "King of kings, Ruler of all the nations, Lord of lords." And the four and twenty elders are casting their crowns at Your feet, and so are all the others—proclaiming that You shall reign forever and ever. You are enthroned upon the praises coming from all these people, and a Voice from On High is saying, "This is My beloved Son, in Whom I am well pleased!"

Officer 1: What a great day this turned out to be!

He: Yes, and it shall never ever end.

Multitude: *Amen!*

WE CALL HER SHILOH

So beautiful and delicate,
a city on a hill.
She leans on her Beloved One
for strength her place to fill.

Her humble walls a manger,
where the sons of God are born.
There prophets speak and apostolic
companies are formed.

Here youth may come, or simple ones,
the Way of Life to seek;
and older ones, who know their God,
in faithful Wisdom speak.

Wise men who seek the Light will come
from countries near and far,
as those who came to Bethlehem
perceived that Guiding Star.

The weary ones, the battle worn
and wounded in the fray—
you give them rest, a healing balm,
and help them on their way.

We all are counting and are sure,
wherever we reside,
His scepter won't depart from you,
while Samuel doth preside!

A WORD ABOUT THE LIVING WORD

I'd like to say something about the Living Word:
Most wonderful thing I've ever heard!
It's a lot more to me than a bunch of books.
And it's a whole lot different than the way it looks.

It's a better way to think and a better way to live.
It's a new way of thinking and a new way to give.
It's a living, breathing body, separated, set apart.
Every member has its function, but together just one heart.

It's the heart of John Stevens, and many others too,
and it is so all inclusive, it includes even you!
It's a life laid down and left at the altar,
and with faith, hope, and love, it will never ever falter.

It's an illustrated story of a way a life should be.
Gives your life a new beginning, though the end you do not see.
Like a child that's filled with wonder, what the next word will reveal,
and the wounds this life has caused us, He will surely, surely heal.

It's unfolding revelation of the Christ we thought we knew,
but we really get to know Him as the works He did we do!
He's not just a suffering Savior, come to save us from our sin,
but the King of a great Kingdom in our hearts to dwell within.

It's a living, breathing Person, sent from God into our world,
and with resurrection power, quenched the darts that Satan's hurled.
He's the image of the Father, Lord of life and death and hell,
King of all that's been created, and our Lord, Emmanuel.

I bow down my heart before you, Living Word, for all You are,
as I walk down here beside You, our relating none can mar.
None can take away the joyful adulation in my heart,
as I hear the words You whisper: "We shall never ever part.

MY SEPTEMBER

Though the days are fast approaching,
the September of my years,
I'll not live in anxious longing,
nor take counsel of my fears.

And as rays of light approach me,
gleaming from the other side,
I will steadfast keep my focus,
while on Earth I must abide.

Many works I have to finish;
many things I have to say;
many friends I must encourage,
ere I reach the perfect Day.

I must free men of Earth's bondage,
bring them to the end of strife.
I must show them how to find You,
guide them to eternal life.

When I hear the sound of laughter,
through the ever-thinning veil,
I'll still wait here till He calls me,
knowing He will never fail.

Soon a brighter Light approaches,
brighter than the noonday sun.
It's the end of my December.
All my work, I'll know, is done.

I'll not doubt, whene'er He whispers
in my ear, "It's time to go."
My frail tent will then be folded.
New life then, with Him, I'll know!

MY PLAN FOR MAN
October 2003

Oh, could it be, in Eden fair
(by substitution you were there)
that I revealed a hidden plan:
to teach you how to be a man?

Though Adam fell, yet I arose,
a hidden plan thus to propose.

He chose the wrong tree, don't you see?
But then I chose a different tree
to purchase back that which was lost.
I paid the price, the total cost!

Now we have man, the creature back.
What does he need, what does he lack?
He still can choose which way to go,
the tempter's way or Mine to know.

There is God's will he can pursue,
exactly as I chose to do.
As second Adam, sent as man,
I came to show the Father's plan.

To walk on water I was led.
I healed the sick and raised the dead.
Now it's your turn to do the same!
By faith and grace, just use My Name.

Not one thing is impossible,
as on that Name you humbly call.
Yes, many sons shall come to birth;
Emmanuel has come to Earth!

SONGS IN THE NIGHT

A silent night was all we had
until You came along,
and broke our darkness with Your light,
our silence with Your song.

Not only angels, now can sing,
and shepherds watch by night.
We, too, can sing and watch for You,
now that we have our sight!

Because You came that Holy Night,
we have a second birth.
And only as we find You so
can there be peace on Earth.

Though darkness and a sepulcher
the Christ could not retain;
the Light still shines, and in our hearts,
You always will remain.

Though angels sang that Holy Night,
and wonderful it seemed,
there is a song they cannot sing:
"The Song of the Redeemed."

When You shall come with trumpet sound,
again our darkness tread,
the sleeping ones, who wait for You
will rise up from the dead.

A multitude awaits the time
that's drawing very nigh,
when night shall end, the Day begin,
with songs we sing, On High!

TODAY

So quietly, in my repose
and long before the sun arose,
a precious gift had come my way.
A treasure? Yes, it's called "Today."

Tomorrow never comes to be,
and yesterday is history.
What I must do is find a way
to do and be what's right Today!

I should have done so many things;
a few regrets my memory brings.
But I'll do yet, without delay,
those things and more! While it's Today.

In vain, I watch the moments fly;
I cannot stop them, though I try.
They turn to years and fade away.
What do I have? I have Today!

I'm waiting for a special Day,
the one that will not fade away—
that one long, joyful, endless Day.
Then it will always be Today.

SILENCE

The forest glade is silent now,
as quietly my knees I bow.
The clouds are frozen in the sky,
and birds are silent as they fly.
The lion's roar has also ceased.
So silent now, the king of beasts!

The solitude is so profound—
like deafness, not a single sound.
For this I seek and this I find,
in the forest of my mind.

So faint, I hear a footstep fall;
or did I hear a sound at all?
Yes, it's the sound I've waited for.
The One Who stills the lion's roar
is wandering through
this forest of my mind!

O come and share this place with me.
Let turmoil cease and silence be.
So quietly let all be still;
He comes to "whosoever will."
Alone He breaks the silence
of the forest in your mind.

THE EVENING ARTIST

The Artist sits with brush in hand;
His canvas is the sky.
And does He paint for everyone,
or just for you and I?

At first the sky's a lighter blue,
pink clouds are here and there,
and then a little darker hue
with streaks like angels' hair.

He borrows fire from yonder sun,
not like the morning haze;
this day must end, not as begun,
but in a glorious blaze!

His royal colors now appear:
purple and gold so bright.
With kingly robes He clothes His sons,
before He brings the night.

Now, one more time, He moves the brush,
the sky grows darker, yet
the beauty of this evening scene
no one could soon forget.

He switches on the stars, before
He leaves the canvas black,
and says to all, "Don't fret, My friends,
tomorrow I'll be back!

"I'll do this painting while I can,
and here's the reason why:
someday this Earth will have an end,
and I'll roll up the sky."

Beyond this earthly sunset lies
a land of endless days.
Then shall the Artist be the scene
on which we love to gaze.

THE BRIDE

Up! From the dust of Earth she comes;
from death we see her rise,
and look on her Beloved One
with pure and holy eyes.

Partaking of mortality,
He came to take her place,
and by one faithful sacrifice,
revealed His love and grace.

"From every tribe and place on Earth,
where mortal men reside,
I sought and found My chosen one
and brought her to My side.

"I gladly gave My life for you,
that you could have a choice.
O answer this one prayer for Me,
and hear My pleading Voice:

"Shake off the dust! Please sit with Me
upon My Father's throne,
and take the place He makes for you,
to be My very own."

The witnesses are gathered now,
a great unnumbered throng.
They cast their crowns down at His feet
and sing the "Victor's Song."

Her linen garments, clean and white,
the wedding guests admire,
were purified and brighter made
through tribulation's fire!

Let men from Earth and those above
lift holy hands as one;
unto the Father, Who unites
the Bride and firstborn Son!

LORD, LET IT BE ME!

If someone could kneel beside You
in Your dark Gethsemane,
then take up their cross and follow,
as You said, "Come follow Me."

Though the path leads up to Calvary
and upon that cruel tree,
someone else could suffer with You,
Lord, let it be me!

When someone should lay their life down
for the sheep You love so dear,
if You're calling for a shepherd,
whom the faintest cry shall hear;

when the lion and the wolf come,
who will then the David be?
I would lean upon Your promise, saying,
Yes, let it be me!

When the Father says to crown You
King of kings and Lord of lords,
the unnumbered host will worship,
shout Your name in one accord!

If someone could kneel beside You
in Your hour of victory
and rejoice with You forever,
Lord, let it be me!
Yes, let it be me!

THE LITTLE TIN CUP

Somewhere on a corner, a poor beggar stands.
About all he owns is the cup in his hands.
A stranger walks by, but no coin He will give.
"Just come home with me now, and see where I live."

"But what of my corner and cup?" I then said.
He said, "I will stand there and beg in your stead!
I am taking your place here, and you can take Mine.
But we must go home first to My place and dine.

"You must meet My Father; He's waiting for Me.
Just who I'll bring with Me, He's waiting to see.
He knows of your corner, yes, *you* and your cup.
Today, from His chalice, He's saying, "Drink up!"

And how does He know me—Your Father, I mean?
"Well, My Father loved you ere His face you've seen.
And your name's engraved in the palms of My hands;
I lift them up to Him and He understands!

But come! Let's go home to your Father and Mine;
there are Letters to read and a paper to sign."

It...it says *I'm adopted!* A place I now share
with You and the Father. *It says I'm an heir!*

"Just sign next to My name. (It's written in red.)
It says that, with Me, you arose from the dead!
And just so you'll know that you're His very own,
He wants you to sit here, with Us on His Throne!"

From a seat on the corner to this marvelous Place,
I stand all amazed, at His wonderful grace.
And just a reminder, lest I get puffed up,
there sits on the mantle my Little Tin Cup.

19

IMMANUEL

You walked upon our waters, deep;
our lame and sick made well.
A Father's Son You are to Him,
to us: Immanuel.

Upon Your cross You bore our sins
and conquered Death and Hell.
Your victor's crown will bear the name:
Our Lord, Immanuel.

With crowns of gold and loving names,
more than our tongues can tell,
to us, the greatest Name of all
is: Our Immanuel.

Into our world the angels came,
with joy they sang, "Noel."
Now from the world, we sing our love
to You, Immanuel!

FILLED AND PURIFIED

What is this rushing mighty wind?
Is it the promise He would send?
In upper rooms we wait for Thee;
Come hear our prayer on bended knee!

As early rain fell upon them,
let latter rain fill us from Him.
They needed much, just to begin;
don't we need more, so near the end?

O let us wait before the Throne.
He'll hear our cry, our desperate groan!
We come to One, who is the same;
He said, "Just call upon My Name."

Show wondrous things, which we know not;
what we believe will be our lot.
With Spirit full, let's be baptized.
Let blinding scales fall from our eyes.

Break up! Break up your fallow ground!
Have ears to hear the joyful sound.
He comes to "whosoever will,"
His wondrous Gift with us to fill.

O bride, for Him be purified;
speak forth the Word, both far and wide:
"The Bridegroom comes," may we declare.
"Your bride is ready, so pure and fair!"

A DREAM, OR JUDGMENT

I'm standing and waiting in front of the door;
how long doesn't matter, for time is no more!
The door partly opens, and there I behold
a room of great portions with carpet of gold.

It was a long carpet, it seemed like a mile.
"Be strong then," I whispered. "At least try to smile."
I walked down that carpet, as I'd lived...*alone*,
facing the Judge on the Great White Throne.

"Does He know me?" I ask. "Does He really know me?"
The books were then opened for all to see.
My deeds were made known for all to read.
(I heard this was coming—I didn't take heed.)

What words could I utter? What could I say?
My tongue had been buried back there, in the clay.
I'm seeing a Face I had seen before;
the One Who had knocked so oft at my door.

My eyes are now pleading: "Consider my state!"
"I'm sorry," He said, "but it's really too late.
The knock was not answered," I heard Him say.
"You said I could wait for another day!

Well, here we are at the end of it all;
and now you are wishing I would hear your call?"
"Please let me go back, for a little while!"
He didn't answer—just gave me a smile.

I woke up, this morning and jumped out of bed.
She said, "You seem happy?" I said, "Yeah, *I'm not dead!*
It's Sunday, besides, so I'll walk up the street.
There's Someone there I've just got to meet!"

But as I reached out, the door to unlock,
I heard a very familiar knock.
I said, " Please come in! Oh, please, do come in!"
He said, *"Okay, glad to see you...again!"*

COMING FOR YOU

Much brighter than the sun
and fairer than the moon;
there stands the Holy One,
Who's coming very soon.

It's Christ who is anointed,
from the dead is risen.
As it was appointed,
preached to those in prison.

Soon we'll see His face,
as Heaven's highest choice.
It's only by His grace
that we have heard His voice.

"O come and follow Me now,"
we have heard Him say.
And opened eyes will see
us walk in endless Day.

Those songs of the redeemed,
we'll sing, and we will shine.
No matter how it seemed,
He'll say to us, "You're Mine."

Ah, such a wondrous story,
a loving thing to do—
to leave the realms of glory
and come for me and you!

WALK ON YOUR STORM

I could not wait upon the shore
to catch a glimpse and nothing more.
Nor on this boat will I rely.
If step out I can but die!

But there is One, mighty to save;
He's out there walking on the wave.
I cried, "Lord, bid me come to You;
the works You do, so must I do."

He bade me, "Come!" And in that hour,
o'er wind and wave I felt the power.
But then I saw those waves reach out;
"I'm sinking, Lord, save Me!" I shout.

He lifted me up and drew me near
and made it very, very clear:
it was my doubts and not the sea,
that was about to swallow me.

If you're in comfort on the shore,
come on! Launch out! There's so much more!
Let us not trust how it may seem;
let's walk with Him. *He is supreme!*

WALKING TOGETHER

I come to you now, Lord Jesus;
take me by the hand, I pray.
Show me how to walk before You;
teach me, Lord, just what to say.

I want to live with You forever,
want to see Your face above,
but I'll walk down here beside You
till I see Your Kingdom love.

Fill me with Your Holy Spirit;
teach me how to walk in grace.
Faith will guide my steps before You
till I see You face to face.

Bring us out of Egypt's bondage;
let the flesh drown in the sea,
nor let murmurs or complaining
break our precious unity.

We will walk in love and mercy,
(as You prayed there in Your Word),
speak Your Word to one another,
dwell in peace and one accord.

WHEN?

When shall I see the Holy One?
When shall I meet the Father's Son?
When shall I hear Him say, "Well done"?
When shall I see Him?

When shall I know as I am known?
When shall be reaped the seed that's sown?
When shall He claim me as His own?
When shall I see Him?

When shall I see Him face to face?
When shall He claim me by His grace
and hold me in His strong embrace?
When shall I see Him?

When darkness turns to realms of light.
When blindness changes into sight
and daybreak banishes the night.
Then shall I see Him!

27

DOWN TO EARTH
For Kate, age four weeks

I wasn't too happy to come here, you know!
Things there were much better than down here below.
One thing was lacking, you know, "up above,"
and down here I found it, it's called Mother's Love.

I needed a father—must have one they say.
So now I have you, Dad, to love every day!
The Martha in Scripture, the Savior did serve,
now Martha's my mother. I do not deserve!

They both love each other; they both love me too.
Our Father in Heaven loves all—even you!

Not only to love them, but others out there,
I came to tell *all men* of our Savior's care.
I'll tell of the wounds in His hands and His feet,
and words from His heart unto them I'll repeat.

I hope they will hear me and stand by His grace,
and see what I saw in His wonderful face.

I'm glad He came here—first to open the Way,
so I could come also and know what to say.
No longer two footprints on Galilee's shore,
but thousands will come, and then many more.

Yes, I'll go where I came from, but until I do,
I'm spending a lifetime down here—with you!

AUTHORITY IS GIVEN

In seeking truth and righteousness,
rejecting Satan's lies;
in faith and quiet confidence,
we never compromise.

The more we see available,
the more we're pressing in,
accepting our forgiveness and
full cleansing from our sin.

Invited to come boldly
before the throne of grace,
we're finding help as promised,
the more we seek His face.

We're seated at His right hand now
and reaching through the veil.
Authority is given us,
so we will never fail.

Though Satan roars against us,
we will not live in fear.
The gates of hell will tremble
as the sons of God draw near!

We're giving earnest warning to
Earth's princes, kings, and powers:
dominion o'er the Earth returns
unto God's sons this hour!

THY KINGDOM COME!

"Thy Kingdom come!" is what we pray,
but what's our expectation?
We know not what to look for;
it's an unfolding revelation.

We know creation's groaning for
revealing of the sons,
but let's not look for others;
let's be the chosen ones.

The Father sent His Son, the King,
who said, "I'll never leave you."
Faith puts the crown upon His head
and says, "Yes, we believe You!"

Jesus once said to Mary,
"Today is not my day!"
By faith, she said to servants,
"*Do* whatever He may say."

Lord, turn this water into wine,
our faith, our expectation:
"Thy Kingdom come!" O King, today,
rule over every nation!

THE LAMP OF ISRAEL

O Lamp of Israel shine your light
within each heart and soul.
We follow in that light you give,
until we reach the goal.

How silent, yet how fervent burns
the Lamp of Israel!
Upon the Earth it gives the Light,
the Father's love to tell.

Your lamp shall not go out by day;
at night you brightly glow,
to lead the faithful in the Way,
the Kingdom path to know.

The luminaries each are lit
from one great Light above.
And standing close in unity,
the Temple glows with love.

Though darkness comes upon the Earth,
your lamp shines bright as day;
our eyes can see each step to take
within the Kingdom way.

Upon the Living Word we see
you shine on every page,
until epistles—Living Ones—
become the Kingdom age!

LOVE'S GREAT LIGHT

When someone loves a man or child,
to them there is no guilt or guile.
It gives them hope. It gives them fame.
It gives them power to do the same.

For passing down through ages long,
from Eden's trees and Earth's first song,
her voice keeps crying, day and night:
"Pass on that flame's eternal Light!"

Earth's greatest gift came with a cost,
when Love's great Man died on that cross.
The gift He gave was Heaven's best.
What we do now is our great test.

To let that flame grow dark and cold
or lift our torch and not withhold!
For some will seek the light of day;
they need your Light to find the way.

The sun may fade and soon be gone;
but Love's great Light shines on and on!

"JUST FOLLOW ME"

Though some may choose the broader way
and find more room—in which to stray!
I'll take the straight and narrow path—
no fear, no pain, no death or wrath.

I'll follow on, where it may lead;
the signs along the Way I'll heed.
Though I may stumble—almost fall,
there is a *name* on which I call.

And since I walk by faith, not sight,
He'll guide me on the Way marked "Right."
They said, "Build up! Cast out each stone!
Make straight the pathway for His own!"

The sound of music, soon I hear;
One dressed in white doth then appear.
In royal robes He comes my way;
My path is now *the King's highway!*

"Just follow Me, in one accord."
I'll follow on; You are my Lord.
He leads me on, no fear or doubts.
"The path ends here: *my Father's house!*"

COME AND DINE!

I'm traveling down life's long highway;
it's getting later in the day.
A sign ahead says, "Roadside Inn."
I need a rest from where I've been.

I need more strength; I need more power;
I'll read the Good Book for an hour.
Then a bite to eat would be real nice,
or just some water might suffice.

The smell of food now fills the air!
I think it's coming from upstairs.
And, as I ascended, to my surprise,
a great room appeared to my weary eyes.

A large table's set with wine and bread;
disciples all gathered with Christ at the head.
He's saying to us, "It's near time to eat,
but before we do, I will wash your feet."

My prayer had been, "Lord, make me clean."
But these dear ones, where had they been?
O yes, they'd traveled the same as I,
the same old road, in years gone by.

They are the ones who penned the Word
I read downstairs; their voices heard!
Now we're together, in one accord
and with one purpose: *to honor our Lord!*

Let's open the windows to all mankind.
We call in His name: "Come and dine, come and dine!
Come sit at His table; His wine and bread eat.
But, most of all, sit and let Him wash your feet!"

Down life's long road, I'll journey on.
My weariness and fears are gone!
The One Who "promised to abide,"
 now travels with me; He's my guide!

I said, "Lord, where does this road end?"
He said, "I'll tell you what, My friend.
With nothing to fear nor any doubts,
this road ends at our Father's house!"

THE SHEPHERD

The ninety and nine were left, you know.
If just one is lost, the Shepherd will go
and seek that one, like you, who was lost.
But let's not forget, it came at great cost!

His own life He gave that others might live,
so, likewise, true shepherds will also give.
Suppose He is placing His heart in *you*,
O seeker of sheep. (What you are, you will do!)

The Shepherd has called us to one sheepfold,
but some are still out in the dark and cold.
They're out there, you know, the chosen ones,
the ones He has chosen to be His sons.

The one whom the wolves are seeking to kill
may be just the one who would do God's will.
Not just to accept His gift that's so free,
but *cry out to be made* what He wants him to be

and willing to do *whatever* He asks.
This heart comes first, before any task.
The Kingdom of God may wait for just one;
that one, O Shepherd, His son, His son!

BEAUTY

Beauty lies between your eyes
and in your heart within.
It also lies in form and shape
and softness of your skin.

"Pretty is as pretty does,"
was said to some fair youth;
but, young or old, it matters not.
It's just the simple truth!

Those seeds of kindness, sown in youth,
bear fruit time can't erase
and show themselves as beauty marks,
etched on an aging face.

Now meekness is the way to reach
that high and lofty goal,
for He will "beautify the meek"
and bless the humble soul.

The flower of youth will fade away
and vanity will cease,
but they who seek the Lord will find
a deep, abiding peace.

THE MATRIMONIAL SEA

I'll not forget that time and date,
November eighth of fifty-eight,
when vows were made and much was said
and "would endure till we were dead."

You, in that short and glorious hour,
gave up that name, that name of Bower,
and in the same agreed to pick
an Irish name, our McCormick.

We launched our boat upon that sea;
the one they call "Matrimony."
Nor did we ask He change the tide,
but only that He lead and guide.

Our little boat, t'would soon be tossed.
"Throw out the anchor or we'll be lost!"
Ah, yes, the Anchor, it holds secure
and grips the Rock that's safe and sure.

How many perish on rock and shoal
without an Anchor, without a goal?

A Lighthouse shines for sailors lost,
who first forgot to count the cost
and launched upon that awesome tide.
How many sank? How many died?

A great Ship waits; I see it there!
The Captain's heart is filled with care
and waits to take us to that shore,
where ships and lives are lost no more.

But we're not ready for Him, you see;
we like this cruise called "Matrimony."

FREEDOM'S SONG
For our thirty-seventh anniversary

I came to you. You came to me.
And for this cause, you were set free,
to soar the heights on eagle's wing,
and with me, Freedom's song to sing.

The eyes of faith alone could see
what was in store for you and me!
In days ahead, it will unfold.
The Story yet has not been told.

As grow the years of some great tree,
so grows the love I have for thee.
And far beyond this vale of tears,
our love will last beyond the years.

For as His Kingdom comes on Earth,
our love can have a second birth.
The partial will be done away
as we rejoice in His new Day.

And being free from death and sin,
we'll sing sweet Freedom's song again!

TO BE WITH YOU

To be with you, and to pursue,
is what I gave my life to do.

As time goes by, we slowly change;
our features seem to rearrange.
No matter, though, it's still today,
and time cannot take that away.

We deal with One Who stays the same
and makes a promise in His name:
we can conform and be like Him!
It's like the new Jerusalem.

The dusty streets are turned to gold—
new life in what had once been old.
Let me look fully in Your face,
and see the work we know as "grace."

A sudden moment, a sudden change,
and once again a rearrange!
Grow old, again? No thanks, no never!
This time it's going to last forever.

I want to see you on that Day,
but, until then, I'm here to stay—
to be with you and to pursue!
It's what I gave my life to do.

TWO DAYS

She went away the other day,
just hopped a plane and flew away!
She went to see her mom and sis;
how could she leave me here like this?

I'm waiting by the phone, you see.
Why don't she call poor lonely me?
Oh yes, she did! I just forgot,
but even so it matters not.

She's been away for two-whole-days!
I walk around as in a haze.
When we decided she would go,
how it would feel I did not know!

"I miss you so," I said, "my dear!"
She said, "How so, since I'm still here?"
"I know, but soon you will be gone,
and I can't see you on the phone!"

"I will be back again, someday,
and you'll forget I went away."
I know it's true; I know it's right.
Why can't I go to sleep at night?

I look to see the night is through.
I see the clock; it's only two!
But soon the sun comes shining in,
and one-more-day, I must begin.

MOTHER'S DAY

Just what it means to be a mom,
I really couldn't say.
But what she does and who she is
deserves more than one day!

What is it like to have a child
and nurture it each day,
to feed, and cloth, and lead it
in the straight and narrow way?

To keep a house, make it a home,
with everything in place,
and at the end of every day,
a smile upon her face?

"A virtuous woman, who can find?"
the proverb man may say.
I'll tell you where to find her;
she lives with us every day!

What can we do for one like this,
who gives and gives and gives?
Let's honor her on Mother's Day
and every day she lives!

MELTED AS ONE

A snowflake forms up in the sky.
We know not when; we know not why.
Each one is made in its own way,
like each man formed out of the clay.

We see them fall and soon forget.
The One Who formed remembers yet!
With tiny droplets, He begins,
like jewels, formed for His own ends.

They fall to Earth and melt away.
"Tis only water," some may say,
but He Who formed them will reply:
"They melt as one, like you and I."

"They're still My flakes and soon will rise,
again be formed up in the skies,
but not to fall upon the ground;
I'll make them jewels here, in My crown."

WINTER'S ARTWORK

The summer's gone, now winter's blast,
her blanket white o'er us is cast.
To me, the snow is kinda neat,
but do we really need three feet?

With scoop in hand, I will defy
the works of Him Who dwells on high.
But soon the One Who is all wise,
my piteous works will compromise
and cover up what I would gain.
But, stubborn me, I'll start again!

Or should I contemplate a while
Who made each flake, mile after mile?
But if I do, she's bound to say,
"Did you, at least, get the driveway?"

My hands are cold; my face is flush.
The Artist has the bigger brush.
The scene is worth at least a look,
though overnight is all it took!

Of course, those hills of old were made
with bigger Hand and bigger Spade,
but me, I'll work, and ere it's night,
throw off this blanket of *snowy white!*

YOUR NAME IS SPRING

Burst forth, O Spring, upon the Earth!
Let every glade be filled.
New life raise up on every hand,
from that which winter killed.

Beneath the frost you waited
with anticipation long.
Now let us hear your joyful voice,
lift up in verdant song!

With open eyes, behold the day,
as on Creation's dawn,
when Earth beheld the light,
as through the eyes of newborn fawn!

Awake the-trees! Let boughs be bent
with leaves and fruit galore.
New creatures romp and flowers bloom
on forest's grassy floor.

You wave your magic wand in Time,
unfrozen life you bring.
The Earth shall join you in your song,
because your name is *Spring*!

THE GEESE

What mystery makes them rise as one,
and mount up to the sky?
Who teaches them which way is south
and just which way to fly?

What conversations do they have?
What language do they speak?
Can knowledge come from feathered fowl
or wisdom from a beak?

In Vs they form their long, long lines,
but one should take the lead.
How, then, do one and all decide
to whom they will take heed?

What Voice shall warn them on their way:
"Unfriendly guns, below!"
and chart a safer course for them,
a better way to go?

Who knows how high they all must fly
to clear the highest peaks?
The One Who formed the mountains high,
in faithful wisdom speaks!

A snowy storm may come their way,
and then what should they do?
Descend unto the ground below,
or should they just pursue?

Majestically, they journey on
to breaking of the day.
Their compass has been true to them,
to lead them on their way!

The biggest question one may ask
is, When have they arrived?
Is there a place upon a map
from which this is derived?

The place of rest for weary wings
was made long, long ago.
And those who seek that peaceful pond
will surely find it so!

THE RIGHTEOUS DRUMMERS

The drummers are drumming;
they're keeping the beat.
They never break ranks in cold or heat.

They go into battle; the beat resounds.
The enemy shudders at the distant sounds.
Though cannons are roaring and men crying out,
they never give heed to the enemy's shout.

Their beat can be heard on a far-off shore;
hearts failing for fear of what's lying in store.
An army with banners to follow their lead
does march to their sound, and no other they heed.

The battle is won, for they know no defeat,
for the enemy hears that persistent beat.

Take heed, ye warmongers, oppressors of men;
the battles will fall to the spirits akin—
to the drummers who drum to the righteous beat
and follow the One Who directs their feet.

LET FREEDOM RING

An eerie silence fills the air.
The roar of cannon once was there.
Is this for what they lived and died,
in peaceful freedom we may abide?

What can we do to help their cause?
One day per year we stop and pause.
We pray for all of those who fell,
although their names we cannot tell.

Much more, I think, we all must do,
not only them, but me and you!
Eternal vigil we must pay.
They did it then; we do it today.

It's true that freedom is not free.
What kind of men, then, must we be?
Tyrants taunt and threaten harm.
For this we must and do bear arms.

This gift is worth most any price.
For some it's ultimate sacrifice,
but those who live must find a way
to pass the torch to the new day.

It will, of course, be up to them
to offer up their life and limb.
The bugle calls to them, as well.
What they will do, we cannot tell.

Though you can't speak, the Late and Soon,
we offer you this precious boon:
Some rest in peace; we shout and sing,
Let freedom ring! Let freedom ring!

AMERICA!

America! America! may ever it be:
"Home of the brave, land of the free."
Yet from thy bosom the prophets call:
"Fulfill God's will, or else you fall!"

The highest honor comes to thee;
end of an age your eyes shall see.
His Kingdom comes, the time is *now!*
We know not what to do nor how.

We just obey the pleading Voice—
no other plans, no other choice.
With labor pains, they come to birth,
the prophets' voices fill the Earth.

They leap the walls and every fence—
barriers fall and each defense.
With torchlike eyes, they light the night,
bringing the ointment to give you sight.

America! America! *He* comes to you;
remake the plans you now pursue.
Fall on your knees and on your face.
Seek for His mercy; seek for His grace.

His plan for you can now unfold;
the half of which has not been told:
a Garden of Eden; world without sin;
peace with your enemies; peace within.

O CANADA!

We looked with awe at majesty
upon thy mountain peaks.
The splendor in thy valleys, too,
in silent beauty speaks.

We saw your Castle in the Sky;
can kings and knights live up so high?
The Hand who made you, you must know,
made us a home down here below.

And those Three Sisters, standing tall,
make us look oh so very small!
The cold wind sweeps their faces fair
and glist'ning snow provides their hair.

Your forests make a verdant house
for great black bear and tiny mouse.
And every creature spends the day,
like children, left alone to play.

And should we speak of field and stream?
A surreal sight—more like a dream!

O Canada! Your silent show
has blest us more than you can know.

About the Author

Don McCormick was born in Colorado, but his family moved to Texas while he was very young. He eventually attended Wayland Baptist College in Plainview, Texas, where he studied for the ministry.

He heard about an evangelist in California, John Stevens, who wanted to see the church return to the New Testament order of worship and participation. Don wanted to help him build that church, called Grace Chapel of South Gate. Other churches were started, and others came into the fellowship, even from other countries. That group of churches came to be called the Living Word Fellowship of Churches.

Seeing people's lives changed and churches come into the New Testament pattern has been a great source of inspiration for Don. His hope is that all who read *The Highest Honor* will be blessed and inspired to move ahead.

Made in the USA
Charleston, SC
26 September 2013